ALL ABOUT L

AN EASY LUNCH COOKBOOK FILLED WITH DELICIOUS LUNCH RECIPES

By
BookSumo Press
Copyright © by Saxonberg Associates

Published by
BookSumo Press, a DBA of Saxonberg Associates
http://www.booksumo.com/

JOIN THE BOOKSUMO PRIVATE READER'S CLUB AND GET A MASSIVE COLLECTION OF 6 COOKBOOKS!

The first set of cookbook is for the lovers of easy cooking.

You will get the "Easy Specialty Cookbook Box Set" for FREE!

This box set includes the following cookbooks:

1. Easy Sushi Cookbook
2. Easy Dump Dinner Cookbook
3. Easy Beans Cookbook

AND for the ethnic and cultural food lovers you will also get the "Easy Cultural Cookbook Box Set" for FREE as well!

This box set includes the following cookbooks:

1. A Kitchen in Morocco
2. Easy Samosas & Pot Pie Recipes
3. The Biryani Bash

Join the group of private readers, and enjoy these cookbooks. This collection is only available for private readers and it's over 400 pages when printed! Plus you will receive fun updates, and musings about food and cooking.

6 Cookbooks. 400+ pages of recipes. Everything delicious and easy.

To get these 6 free books just stay to the end of this cookbook and follow the directions at the back!

ABOUT THE AUTHOR.

BookSumo Press is a publisher of unique, easy, and healthy cookbooks.

Our cookbooks span all topics and all subjects. If you want a deep dive into the possibilities of cooking with any type of ingredient. Then BookSumo Press is your go to place for robust yet simple and delicious cookbooks and recipes. Whether you are looking for great tasting pressure cooker recipes or authentic ethic and cultural food. BookSumo Press has a delicious and easy cookbook for you.

With simple ingredients, and even simpler step-by-step instructions BookSumo cookbooks get everyone in the kitchen chefing delicious meals.

BookSumo is an independent publisher of books operating in the beautiful Garden State (NJ) and our team of chefs and kitchen experts are here to teach, eat, and be merry!

INTRODUCTION

Welcome to *The Effortless Chef Series*! Thank you for taking the time to purchase this cookbook.

Come take a journey into the delights of easy cooking. The point of this cookbook and all BookSumo Press cookbooks is to exemplify the effortless nature of cooking simply.

In this book we focus on delicious Lunch recipes. You will find that even though the recipes are simple, the taste of the dishes are quite amazing.

So will you take an adventure in simple cooking? If the answer is yes please consult the table of contents to find the dishes you are most interested in.

Once you are ready, jump right in and start cooking.

— BookSumo Press

TABLE OF CONTENTS

ANY ISSUES? CONTACT US

If you find that something important to you is missing from this book please contact us at info@booksumo.com.

We will take your concerns into consideration when the 2nd edition of this book is published. And we will keep you updated!

— BookSumo Press

LEGAL NOTES

COMMON ABBREVIATIONS

cup(s)	C.
tablespoon	tbsp
teaspoon	tsp
ounce	oz.
pound	lb

*All units used are standard American measurements

CHAPTER 1: EASY LUNCH RECIPES

TURKEY, SUNDRIED TOMATO, BASIL PANINI

Ingredients

- 4 Dinner Rolls, split
- Plain or sundried tomato mayonnaise (see below)
- 4 slices roast turkey or ham
- 4 slices Swiss, Monterey Jack, or Gruyere cheese
- 8 small slices red onion
- 1 C. fresh spinach leaves or several fresh basil leaves(optional)
- Salt and freshly ground black pepper
- Butter

Tomato Mayo:

- 1/4 C. mayonnaise
- 2 finely chopped sundried tomatoes
- Salt and freshly ground black pepper

Directions

- Spread mayonnaise and place all the ingredients except over roll.
- Grill sandwich on the Panini machine for seven minutes (three minutes if you are using a pan) after spreading some butter on the top and bottom.
- Whisk all the ingredients for mayonnaise together and set it aside for later use.

Serving: 4

Timing Information:

Preparation	Cooking	Total Time
10 mins	10 mins	20 mins

Nutritional Information:

Calories	464 kcal
Carbohydrates	40.8 g
Cholesterol	60 mg
Fat	26.6 g
Fiber	3.8 g
Protein	17.4 g
Sodium	936 mg

* Percent Daily Values are based on a 2,000 calorie diet.

HUMMUS, EGGPLANT, MOZZARELLA PANINI

Ingredients

- 1 baby eggplant, cut into 1/4-inch slices
- salt and ground black pepper to taste
- 1/4 C. olive oil, divided
- 1 loaf flat bread, sliced horizontally and cut into 4 equal pieces
- 1/2 (12 oz) jar roasted red bell peppers, drained and sliced
- 4 oz shredded mozzarella cheese
- 1/4 C. roasted garlic hummus

Directions

- Coat eggplant slices with salt and pepper before letting it stand as it is for two minutes.
- Cook eggplant in batches in hot olive oil for about three minutes each side.
- Put eggplant, mozzarella cheese and red pepper over bread before spreading some hummus over the top piece of bread.
- Now grill these Paninis on a preheated Panini press for about 7 minutes or until the cheese has melted.

Serving: 1

Timing Information:

Preparation	Cooking	Total Time
15 mins	15 mins	30 mins

Nutritional Information:

Calories	401 kcal
Carbohydrates	41.5 g
Cholesterol	18 mg
Fat	21.7 g
Fiber	5.2 g
Protein	15.7 g
Sodium	625 mg

* Percent Daily Values are based on a 2,000 calorie diet.

CHICKEN, MONTEREY, BASIL PESTO PANINI

Ingredients

- 1 focaccia bread, quartered
- 1/2 C. prepared basil pesto
- 1 C. diced cooked chicken
- 1/2 C. diced green bell pepper
- 1/4 C. diced red onion
- 1 C. shredded Monterey Jack cheese

Directions

- Heat up your Panini grill according to the instruction of the manufacturer.
- Spread pesto over each half of focaccia bread before putting chicken, cheese, bell pepper and onion over the lower half, and closing it up to make a sandwich.
- Cook this Panini in the preheated grill for about 5 minutes or until the outside is golden brown.

Serving: 4

Timing Information:

Preparation	Cooking	Total Time
15 mins	5 mins	20 mins

Nutritional Information:

Calories	641 kcal
Carbohydrates	60.9 g
Cholesterol	61 mg
Fat	29.4 g
Fiber	4.4 g
Protein	32.4 g
Sodium	1076 mg

* Percent Daily Values are based on a 2,000 calorie diet.

CHEDDAR, CHIPOTLE, CAESAR, BACON PANINI

Ingredients

- 2 slices sourdough bread
- 1/4 C. Caesar salad dressing
- 1 cooked chicken breast, diced
- 1/2 C. shredded Cheddar cheese
- 1 tbsp bacon bits, optional
- 1 1/2 tsps chipotle chili powder, or to taste
- 2 tbsps softened butter

Directions

- Heat up your Panini grill according to the instruction of the manufacturer.
- Spread Caesar dressing over each half of the bread before putting chicken, cheddar cheese, bacon bits and chipotle chili powder over the lower half, and closing it up to make a sandwich.
- Put some butter on top and cook this Panini in the preheated grill for about 4 minutes or until the outside is golden brown.

Serving: 1

Timing Information:

Preparation	Cooking	Total Time
10 mins	5 mins	15 mins

Nutritional Information:

Calories	1243 kcal
Carbohydrates	31.9 g
Cholesterol	312 mg
Fat	83.9 g
Fiber	1.5 g
Protein	85.7 g
Sodium	1813 mg

* Percent Daily Values are based on a 2,000 calorie diet.

ROMANO, BASIL, CHICKEN, CAESAR PANINI

Ingredients

- 1/4 C. packed fresh basil leaves
- 1/4 C. olive oil
- 4 cloves garlic, diced
- 2 tbsps grated Romano cheese
- 1 tsp dried oregano
- 1 tsp ground black pepper
- 2 skinless, boneless chicken breast halves
- 2 tbsps creamy Caesar salad dressing
- 6 slices Italian bread with sesame seeds (Scali)
- 1/2 C. shredded iceberg lettuce
- 2 thin slices smoked mozzarella

Directions

- Heat up your grill and put some oil on the grate
- Blend a mixture of basil, oregano, oil, garlic, Romano cheese and pepper in a blender until smooth.
- Now grill chicken on the preheated grill for about 5 minutes each side.

- Spread Caesar dressing over the bread and put lettuce before putting additional slice of bread over it.
- Now put cooked chicken breast and smoked mozzarella before closing it up to make a sandwich.
- Cook this Panini in the preheated grill for about three minutes or until the outside is golden brown.

Serving: 2

Timing Information:

Preparation	Cooking	Total Time
20 mins	16 mins	36 mins

Nutritional Information:

Calories	587 kcal
Carbohydrates	20 g
Cholesterol	85 mg
Fat	41.5 g
Fiber	1.8 g
Protein	32.5 g
Sodium	523 mg

* Percent Daily Values are based on a 2,000 calorie diet.

SOURDOUGH, PROVOLONE, PESTO PANINI

Ingredients

- 1/2 C. Extra Virgin Olive Oil
- 8 slices sourdough bread
- 1/4 C. pesto
- 16 thin slices Provolone cheese
- 12 thin slices prosciutto
- 4 whole, roasted red peppers, julienned

Directions

- Heat up your Panini grill according to the instruction of the manufacturer.
- Spread pesto over each half of the bread before putting ½ of cheese, prosciutto, pepper strips and the remaining cheese over the lower half, and closing it up to make a sandwich.
- Put some butter on top and cook this Panini in the preheated grill for about 4 minutes or until the outside is golden brown.

Serving: 4

Timing Information:

Preparation	Cooking	Total Time
15 mins	4 mins	19 mins

Nutritional Information:

Calories	798 kcal
Carbohydrates	27.4 g
Cholesterol	76 mg
Fat	63.9 g
Fiber	2.1 g
Protein	31 g
Sodium	1754 mg

* Percent Daily Values are based on a 2,000 calorie diet.

Avocado, Turkey, Spinach, Ciabatta

Ingredients

- 4 slices artisan bread such as ciabatta
- 2 tsps honey Dijon salad dressing
- 1/2 C. baby spinach leaves
- 1/4 lb sliced oven-roasted deli turkey breast
- 1/4 red onion, cut into strips
- 1 ripe avocado from Mexico, peeled, pitted and thickly sliced
- Salt and pepper to taste
- 1/4 C. crumbled soft goat cheese
- Non-stick cooking spray

Directions

- Heat up your Panini grill according to the instruction of the manufacturer.
- Spread honey Dijon dressing, spinach leaves, turkey breast and red onion over lower half of the bread before putting avocado slices, salt, pepper and goat cheese over the upper half, and closing it up to make a sandwich.

- Put some butter on top and cook this Panini in the preheated grill for about 8 minutes or until the outside is golden brown.

Serving: 2

Timing Information:

Preparation	Cooking	Total Time
10 mins	10 mins	20 mins

Nutritional Information:

Calories	469 kcal
Carbohydrates	45.5 g
Cholesterol	37 mg
Fat	23.8 g
Fiber	8.5 g
Protein	22.1 g
Sodium	1250 mg

* Percent Daily Values are based on a 2,000 calorie diet.

THE BEST PANINI DIP

Ingredients

- 1 tbsp mayonnaise
- 1 1/2 tsps hot pepper sauce
- 2 tsps garlic powder

Directions

- Combine all the ingredients very thoroughly in a bowl before refrigerating it for at least an hour.
- Serve with any Panini.

Serving: 1

Timing Information:

Preparation	Cooking	Total Time
5 mins		5 mins

Nutritional Information:

Calories	118 kcal
Carbohydrates	4.6 g
Cholesterol	5 mg
Fat	11 g
Fiber	0.6 g
Protein	1.1 g
Sodium	265 mg

* Percent Daily Values are based on a 2,000 calorie diet.

YOGURT, PARMESAN, BASIL, TURKEY PANINI

Ingredients

- 3 tbsps reduced-fat mayonnaise
- 2 tbsps nonfat plain yogurt
- 2 tbsps shredded Parmesan cheese
- 2 tbsps chopped fresh basil
- 1 tsp lemon juice
- Freshly ground pepper to taste
- 8 slices whole-wheat bread
- 8 oz thinly sliced reduced-sodium deli turkey
- 8 tomato slices
- 2 tsps canola oil

Directions

- Heat up your Panini grill according to the instruction of the manufacturer.
- Spread a mixture of mayonnaise, lemon juice, yogurt, Parmesan, basil and pepper over each half of the bread before putting turkey and tomato slices over the lower half, and closing it up to make a sandwich.

- Put some butter on top and cook this Panini in the preheated grill for about 4 minutes or until the outside is golden brown.

Serving: 4

Timing Information:

Preparation	Cooking	Total Time
15 mins	10 mins	25 mins

Nutritional Information:

Calories	279 kcal
Carbohydrates	26.9 g
Cholesterol	31 mg
Fat	9.7 g
Fiber	4.4 g
Protein	22.1 g
Sodium	673 mg

* Percent Daily Values are based on a 2,000 calorie diet.

CHICKEN BREAST, ZUCCHINI, PEPPER PANINI

Ingredients

- 1/2 C. Tuscan Dressing
- 2 (4 oz) boneless skinless chicken breast halves
- 1 red pepper, cut into strips
- 1 small zucchini, cut lengthwise in half, then sliced crosswise
- 4 slices Italian bread
- 1/2 C. KRAFT Shredded Low-Moisture Part-Skim Mozzarella Cheese
- 2 tbsps chopped fresh basil

Directions

- Coat a mixture of vegetables and chicken with dressing before refrigerating it for at least thirty minutes.
- Heat up your Panini grill according to the instruction of the manufacturer.
- Cook chicken and vegetables over medium heat in a skillet for about 10 minutes or until tender.
- Now fill up the bread slices with chicken, vegetables, basil and cheese.

- Put some dressing on top of the bread and cook this Panini in the preheated grill for about five minutes or until the outside is golden brown.

Serving: 2

Timing Information:

Preparation	Cooking	Total Time
10 mins	35 mins	45 mins

Nutritional Information:

Calories	597 kcal
Carbohydrates	32.5 g
Cholesterol	98 mg
Fat	34.1 g
Fiber	3 g
Protein	36.3 g
Sodium	979 mg

* Percent Daily Values are based on a 2,000 calorie diet.

ALMOND DIJON SALAD

Ingredients

- 1 C. sliced almonds
- 3 tbsps red wine vinegar
- 1/3 C. olive oil
- 1/4 C. fresh cranberries
- 1 tbsp Dijon mustard
- 1/2 tsp minced garlic
- 1/2 tsp salt
- 1/2 tsp ground black pepper
- 2 tbsps water
- 1/2 red onion, thinly sliced
- 4 oz. crumbled blue cheese
- 1 lb mixed salad greens

Directions

- Set your oven to 375 degrees before doing anything else.
- Place all your almonds on a cookie sheet and bake them for 7 mins in the oven
- Now puree the following with a food processor: water, vinegar, pepper, oil, salt, garlic, and mustard.

- Get a bowl, combine: the vinegar mix, baked almonds, greens, blue cheese, and onions.
- Enjoy.

Amount per serving (8 total)

Timing Information:

Preparation	15 m
Cooking	5 m
Total Time	20 m

Nutritional Information:

Calories	218 kcal
Fat	19.2 g
Carbohydrates	6.2g
Protein	6.5 g
Cholesterol	11 mg
Sodium	405 mg

* Percent Daily Values are based on a 2,000 calorie diet.

SEATTLE SALAD

Ingredients

- 1/2 C. freshly squeezed lemon juice
- 1/4 C. extra-virgin olive oil
- 2 tsps Dijon mustard
- salt and ground black pepper to taste
- 5 C. water
- 2 C. uncooked wild rice
- 1 tsp butter
- 4 C. finely sliced red cabbage
- 2 large red bell peppers - seeded, cored, and diced
- 2 bulbs fennel, trimmed and diced
- 2 bunches kale, leaves stripped from stems and torn into pieces
- 1/4 lemon, juiced, or to taste

Directions

- Get a bowl, combine: pepper, half C. lemon juice, Dijon, olive oil, and salt.
- Now get your wild rice boiling in water. Once it is boiling add the butter, place a lid on the pot, set the heat to low, and let the rice gently cook for 40 mins.

- Now remove any liquids and cook everything for 7 more mins until no liquid remains.
- Let the rice lose its heat then stir it.
- Get a 2nd bowl, combine: dressing, cabbage, fennel, and bell peppers.
- Lay your kale on top then add the wild rice over the kale.
- Let the salad sit for 7 mins before stirring.
- Now add some extra lemon juice then serve.
- Enjoy.

Amount per serving (12 total)

Timing Information:

Preparation	15 m
Cooking	35 m
Total Time	1 h

Nutritional Information:

Calories	211 kcal
Fat	6 g
Carbohydrates	35.2g
Protein	7.6 g
Cholesterol	< 1 mg
Sodium	< 103 mg

* Percent Daily Values are based on a 2,000 calorie diet.

AMERICAN POTATO SALAD

Ingredients

- 5 potatoes
- 3 eggs
- 1 C. diced celery
- 1/2 C. diced onion
- 1/2 C. sweet pickle relish
- 1/4 tsp garlic salt
- 1/4 tsp celery salt
- 1 tbsp prepared mustard
- ground black pepper to taste
- 1/4 C. mayonnaise

Directions

- Boil your potatoes in water and salt for 20 mins. Then remove the skins and chunk them.
- Now get your eggs boiling in water.
- Once the water is boiling, place a lid on the pot, and shut the heat.
- Let the eggs sit for 15 mins. Then once they have cooled remove the shells, and dice them.

- Get a bowl, combine: mayo, potatoes, pepper, eggs, mustard, celery, celery salt, onions, garlic, and relish.
- Place a covering of plastic on the mix and put everything in the fridge until it is cold.
- Enjoy.

Amount per serving (8 total)

Timing Information:

Preparation	45 m
Cooking	15 m
Total Time	1 h

Nutritional Information:

Calories	206 kcal
Fat	7.6 g
Carbohydrates	30.5g
Protein	5.5 g
Cholesterol	72 mg
Sodium	335 mg

* Percent Daily Values are based on a 2,000 calorie diet.

TARRAGON WILD RICE SALAD

Ingredients

- 1 1/2 C. uncooked wild rice
- 6 C. water
- 1/3 C. tarragon vinegar
- 3 tbsps Dijon mustard
- 1 tbsp white sugar
- 1 tsp salt
- 1 clove garlic, minced
- 1 tsp dried tarragon, crumbled
- 1/2 tsp black pepper
- 1/2 tsp crushed red pepper flakes
- 2/3 C. safflower oil
- 3 C. cubed cooked chicken
- 1 C. sliced celery
- 1/2 C. diced fresh parsley
- 1/2 C. sliced green onion
- 1/2 lb sugar snap peas, strings removed
- 1/2 C. toasted slivered almonds

Directions

- Get your rice boiling in water, place a lid on the pot, set the heat to low, and let the rice cook for 35 mins.
- Remove any extra liquids, and stir the rice.
- Let the rice continue to cook for 7 more mins to remove all the liquids. Then add the rice to a bowl.
- Get a 2nd bowl, combine: pepper flakes, vinegar, black pepper, mustard, tarragon, sugar, garlic, and salt.
- Add the safflower oil and whisk the contents until everything is smooth.
- Now add the following to your rice: green onions, chicken, parsley, and celery.
- Add in the wet oil mix then stir everything.
- Place a covering of plastic over the mix and put everything in the fridge for 5 hrs.
- Now begin to boil your peas in water and salt for 1 min.
- Remove the liquids and run them under cold water. Once the peas are chilled slice them diagonally.
- Combine the almonds and the peas with the rice mix and stir the contents evenly then serve the salad.
- Enjoy.

Amount per serving (10 total)

Timing Information:

Preparation	25 m
Cooking	20 m
Total Time	5 h 15 m

Nutritional Information:

Calories	326 kcal
Fat	20.7 g
Carbohydrates	19.2g
Protein	15.9 g
Cholesterol	32 mg
Sodium	390 mg

* Percent Daily Values are based on a 2,000 calorie diet.

Quinoa Pepper Salad

Ingredients

- 1 tsp canola oil
- 1 tbsp minced garlic
- 1/4 C. diced (yellow or purple) onion
- 2 1/2 C. water
- 2 tsps salt, or to taste
- 1/4 tsp ground black pepper
- 2 C. quinoa
- 3/4 C. diced fresh tomato
- 3/4 C. diced carrots
- 1/2 C. diced yellow bell pepper
- 1/2 C. diced cucumber
- 1/2 C. frozen corn kernels, thawed
- 1/4 C. diced red onion
- 1 1/2 tbsps diced fresh cilantro
- 1 tbsp diced fresh mint
- 1 tsp salt
- 1/4 tsp ground black pepper
- 2 tbsps olive oil
- 3 tbsps balsamic vinegar

Directions

- Stir fry 1/4 C. of onions and garlic in canola for 7 mins. Then add in: 1/4 tsp black pepper, water, 2 tsps salt.
- Get everything boiling then add in the quinoa.
- Place a lid on the pot, set the heat to low, and let the quinoa cook for 22 mins.
- Remove any excess liquids, place the mix in a bowl, and put everything in the fridge until it is cold, with a covering of plastic.
- Once the quinoa is cooled combine it with the following: 1/4 tsp black pepper, 1/4 C. red onions, 1 tsp salt, tomato, mint, corn, cilantro, carrots, cucumber, and bell peppers.
- Top the mix with balsamic and olive oil then stir the contents evenly.
- Enjoy.

Amount per serving (12 total)

Timing Information:

Preparation	20 m
Cooking	25 m
Total Time	1 h 30 m

Nutritional Information:

Calories	148 kcal
Fat	4.5 g
Carbohydrates	22.9g
Protein	4.6 g
Cholesterol	0 mg
Sodium	592 mg

* Percent Daily Values are based on a 2,000 calorie diet.

Asparagus Salad

Ingredients

- 1 lb fresh green beans, trimmed and cut into bite-size pieces
- 1 tbsp extra-virgin olive oil
- 1 lb fresh asparagus, trimmed and cut into bite-size pieces
- 1 tbsp extra-virgin olive oil
- 1/2 red onion, diced
- 2 C. cherry tomatoes, halved
- 1/4 C. diced fresh parsley
- kosher salt to taste
- ground black pepper to taste

Directions

- Set your oven to 400 degrees before doing anything else.
- Get a bowl, combine: olive oil (1 tbsp) and green beans.
- Layer the beans onto a cookie sheet and bake everything in the oven for 12 mins.
- Now combine your asparagus with 1 tbsp of olive oil, in the same bowl, then layer them on the same cookie sheet with the green beans.
- Cook the asparagus and beans for 12 more mins.

- Now in the same bowl, combine: parsley, black pepper, green beans, cherry tomatoes, kosher salt, asparagus, and red onions.
- Enjoy.

Amount per serving (8 total)

Timing Information:

Preparation	15 m
Cooking	20 m
Total Time	35 m

Nutritional Information:

Calories	71 kcal
Fat	3.7 g
Carbohydrates	8.8g
Protein	2.7 g
Cholesterol	0 mg
Sodium	59 mg

* Percent Daily Values are based on a 2,000 calorie diet.

Ranch Pasta Salad

Ingredients

- 1 (12 oz.) package uncooked tri-color rotini pasta
- 10 slices turkey bacon
- 1 C. mayonnaise
- 3 tbsps dry ranch salad dressing mix
- 1/4 tsp garlic powder
- 1/2 tsp garlic pepper
- 1/2 C. milk, or as needed
- 1 large tomato, diced
- 1 (4.25 oz.) can sliced black olives
- 1 C. shredded sharp Cheddar cheese

Directions

- Boil your pasta in water and salt for 9 mins, then remove the liquids.
- Stir fry your bacon then break it into pieces once it becomes crispy.
- Get a bowl, combine: garlic pepper, mayo, garlic powder, ranch dressing mix, and milk.
- Stir the contents then add in: cheese, rotini, black olives, bacon, and tomatoes.

- Stir the contents again until everything is smooth then place a covering of plastic around the bowl and put everything in the fridge for 65 mins.
- If the salad is too dry add a bit more milk, if needed.
- Enjoy.

Amount per serving (10 total)

Timing Information:

Preparation	10 m
Cooking	15 m
Total Time	1 h 25 m

Nutritional Information:

Calories	336 kcal
Fat	26.8 g
Carbohydrates	14.9g
Protein	9.3 g
Cholesterol	31 mg
Sodium	691 mg

* Percent Daily Values are based on a 2,000 calorie diet.

Strawberry Sesame Salad

Ingredients

- 2 tbsps sesame seeds
- 1 tbsp poppy seeds
- 1/2 C. white sugar
- 1/2 C. olive oil
- 1/4 C. distilled white vinegar
- 1/4 tsp paprika
- 1/4 tsp Worcestershire sauce
- 1 tbsp minced onion
- 10 oz. fresh spinach - rinsed, dried and torn into bite-size pieces
- 1 quart strawberries - cleaned, hulled and sliced
- 1/4 C. almonds, blanched and slivered

Directions

- Get a bowl, combine: onion, sesame seeds, Worcestershire, poppy seeds, paprika, sugar, vinegar, and olive oil.
- Place a covering of plastic around the bowl, and put everything in the fridge for 65 mins.

- Get a 2nd bowl, combine: almonds, spinach, and strawberries.
- Combine both bowls and place the combined mix in the fridge for 20 mins.
- Enjoy.

Amount per serving (4 total)

Timing Information:

Preparation	
Cooking	10 m
Total Time	1 h 10 m

Nutritional Information:

Calories	491 kcal
Fat	35.2 g
Carbohydrates	42.9g
Protein	6 g
Cholesterol	0 mg
Sodium	63 mg

* Percent Daily Values are based on a 2,000 calorie diet.

MEDITERRANEAN SALAD

Ingredients

- 3 cucumbers, seeded and sliced
- 1 1/2 C. crumbled feta cheese
- 1 C. black olives, pitted and sliced
- 3 C. diced roma tomatoes
- 1/3 C. diced oil packed sun-dried tomatoes, drained, oil reserved
- 1/2 red onion, sliced

Directions

- Get a bowl, combine: 2 tbsps sun dried tomato oil, red onions, cucumbers, sundried tomatoes, feta, roma tomatoes, and olives.
- Place a covering of plastic around the bowl and put everything in the fridge until it is cold.
- Enjoy.

Amount per serving (8 total)

Timing Information:

Preparation	
Cooking	10 m
Total Time	10 m

Nutritional Information:

Calories	131 kcal
Fat	8.8 g
Carbohydrates	9.3g
Protein	5.5 g
Cholesterol	25 mg
Sodium	486 mg

* Percent Daily Values are based on a 2,000 calorie diet.

CRANBERRY SALAD

Ingredients

- 1 tbsp butter
- 3/4 C. almonds, blanched and slivered
- 1 lb spinach, rinsed and torn into bite-size pieces
- 1 C. dried cranberries
- 2 tbsps toasted sesame seeds
- 1 tbsp poppy seeds
- 1/2 C. white sugar
- 2 tsps minced onion
- 1/4 tsp paprika
- 1/4 C. white wine vinegar
- 1/4 C. cider vinegar
- 1/2 C. vegetable oil

Directions

- Toast your almonds in butter for 7 mins then place them to the side.
- Get a bowl, combine: veggie oil, sesame seeds, cider vinegar, poppy seeds, wine vinegar, sugar, paprika, and onions.

- Combine in the cranberries, almonds, and spinach and toss the contents.
- Enjoy.

Amount per serving (8 total)

Timing Information:

Preparation	10 m
Cooking	10 m
Total Time	20 m

Nutritional Information:

Calories	338 kcal
Fat	23.5 g
Carbohydrates	30.4g
Protein	4.9 g
Cholesterol	4 mg
Sodium	58 mg

* Percent Daily Values are based on a 2,000 calorie diet.

MEXICAN SALAD

Ingredients

- 1 (15 oz.) can black beans, rinsed and drained
- 1 (15 oz.) can kidney beans, drained
- 1 (15 oz.) can cannellini beans, drained and rinsed
- 1 green bell pepper, diced
- 1 red bell pepper, diced
- 1 (10 oz.) package frozen corn kernels
- 1 red onion, diced
- 1/2 C. olive oil
- 1/2 C. red wine vinegar
- 2 tbsps fresh lime juice
- 1 tbsp lemon juice
- 2 tbsps white sugar
- 1 tbsp salt
- 1 clove crushed garlic
- 1/4 C. diced fresh cilantro
- 1/2 tbsp ground cumin
- 1/2 tbsp ground black pepper
- 1 dash hot pepper sauce
- 1/2 tsp chili powder

Directions

- Get a bowl, combine: red onions, beans, frozen corn, and bell pepper.
- Get a 2nd bowl, combine: black pepper, olive oil, garlic, chili powder, cumin, red vinegar, salt, hot sauce, cilantro, lime juice, sugar, and lemon juice.
- Now combine both bowls, and put everything in the fridge until it is cold.
- Enjoy.

Amount per serving (8 total)

Timing Information:

Preparation	
Cooking	15 m
Total Time	1 h 15 m

Nutritional Information:

Calories	334 kcal
Fat	14.8 g
Carbohydrates	41.7g
Protein	11.2 g
Cholesterol	0 mg
Sodium	1159 mg

* Percent Daily Values are based on a 2,000 calorie diet.

MAGGIE'S MACARONI SALAD

Ingredients

- 4 C. uncooked elbow macaroni
- 1 C. mayonnaise
- 1/4 C. distilled white vinegar
- 2/3 C. white sugar
- 2 1/2 tbsps prepared yellow mustard
- 1 1/2 tsps salt
- 1/2 tsp ground black pepper
- 1 large onion, diced
- 2 stalks celery, diced
- 1 green bell pepper, seeded and diced
- 1/4 C. grated carrot
- 2 tbsps diced pimento peppers

Directions

- Boil your macaroni in water and salt for 9 mins then remove the liquids.
- Get a bowl, combine: macaroni, onions, pimentos, celery, carrots, black pepper, mayo, salt, green peppers, vinegar, mustard, and sugar.

- Place a covering of plastic around the bowl and put everything in the fridge for 5 hrs.
- Enjoy.

Amount per serving (10 total)

Timing Information:

Preparation	20 m
Cooking	10 m
Total Time	4 h 30 m

Nutritional Information:

Calories	390 kcal
Fat	18.7 g
Carbohydrates	49.3g
Protein	6.8 g
Cholesterol	8 mg
Sodium	529 mg

* Percent Daily Values are based on a 2,000 calorie diet.

CLASSICAL POTATO SALAD

Ingredients

- 2 lbs clean, scrubbed new red potatoes
- 6 eggs
- 1 lb turkey bacon
- 1 onion, finely diced
- 1 stalk celery, finely diced
- 2 C. mayonnaise
- salt and pepper to taste

Directions

- Boil your potatoes in water and salt for 20 mins then remove the liquids.
- Once the potatoes are no longer hot, chop them, with the skins.
- Now get your eggs boiling in water for 60 secs, place a lid on the pot, and shut the heat.
- Let the eggs sit for 15 mins. Then remove the shells and dice them.
- Stir fry your bacon until it is crispy then break it into pieces.

- Get a bowl, combine: black pepper, celery, salt, eggs, mayo, onion, and bacon.
- Place a covering of plastic around the bowl and put everything in the fridge for 65 mins.
- Enjoy.

Amount per serving (12 total)

Timing Information:

Preparation	
Cooking	1 h
Total Time	2 h

Nutritional Information:

Calories	430 kcal
Fat	36.9 g
Carbohydrates	16.2g
Protein	9.5 g
Cholesterol	121 mg
Sodium	536 mg

* Percent Daily Values are based on a 2,000 calorie diet.

EASY SPINACH SALAD

Ingredients

- 2 bunches spinach, rinsed and torn into bite-size pieces
- 4 C. sliced strawberries
- 1/2 C. vegetable oil
- 1/4 C. white wine vinegar
- 1/2 C. white sugar
- 1/4 tsp paprika
- 2 tbsps sesame seeds
- 1 tbsp poppy seeds

Directions

- Get a bowl, combine: strawberries and spinach.
- Get a 2nd bowl, combine: poppy seeds, oil, sesame seeds, vinegar, paprika, and sugar.
- Combine both bowls then serve the salad.
- Enjoy.

Amount per serving (8 total)

Timing Information:

Preparation	
Cooking	10 m
Total Time	10 m

Nutritional Information:

Calories	235 kcal
Fat	15.9 g
Carbohydrates	22.8g
Protein	3.6 g
Cholesterol	0 mg
Sodium	69 mg

* Percent Daily Values are based on a 2,000 calorie diet.

PECAN CHICKEN SALAD

Ingredients

- 4 C. cubed, cooked chicken meat
- 1 C. mayonnaise
- 1 tsp paprika
- 1 1/2 C. dried cranberries
- 1 C. diced celery
- 2 green onions, diced
- 1/2 C. minced green bell pepper
- 1 C. diced pecans
- 1 tsp seasoning salt
- ground black pepper to taste

Directions

- Get a bowl, combine: seasoned salt, paprika, and mayo. Get this mix smooth then add in: the nuts, celery, onion, bell peppers, and cranberries.
- Mix everything again then add the chicken and black pepper.
- Place the contents in the fridge for 65 mins then serve.
- Enjoy.

Amount per serving (12 total)

Timing Information:

Preparation	
Cooking	15 m
Total Time	15 m

Nutritional Information:

Calories	315 kcal
Fat	23.1 g
Carbohydrates	15.2g
Protein	13.9 g
Cholesterol	42 mg
Sodium	213 mg

* Percent Daily Values are based on a 2,000 calorie diet.

PEAR AND CHEESE SALAD

Ingredients

- 1 head leaf lettuce, torn into bite-size pieces
- 3 pears - peeled, cored and diced
- 5 oz. Roquefort cheese, crumbled
- 1 avocado - peeled, pitted, and diced
- 1/2 C. thinly sliced green onions
- 1/4 C. white sugar
- 1/2 C. pecans
- 1/3 C. olive oil
- 3 tbsps red wine vinegar
- 1 1/2 tsps white sugar
- 1 1/2 tsps prepared mustard
- 1 clove garlic, diced
- 1/2 tsp salt
- fresh ground black pepper to taste

Directions

- Toast your pecans and 1/4 C. of sugar, while stirring, until the sugar melts and coats the pecans.
- Then place the pecans on some parchment paper.

- Blend the following in a blender until smooth: pepper, oil, salt, 1.5 tsp sugar, diced garlic, and mustard.
- Get a bowl, combine: green onions, lettuce, avocados, pears, blue cheese, and dressing mix.
- Stir the contents then add in your pecans.
- Enjoy.

Amount per serving (6 total)

Timing Information:

Preparation	20 m
Cooking	10 m
Total Time	30 m

Nutritional Information:

Calories	426 kcal
Fat	31.6 g
Carbohydrates	33.1g
Protein	8 g
Cholesterol	21 mg
Sodium	654 mg

* Percent Daily Values are based on a 2,000 calorie diet.

Zucchini, Chicken, Mushrooms, and Swiss Brown Rice

Ingredients

- 1/3 C. brown rice
- 1 C. vegetable broth
- 1 tbsp olive oil
- 1/3 C. diced onion
- 1 medium zucchini, thinly sliced
- 2 cooked skinless boneless chicken breast halves, chopped
- 1/2 C. sliced mushrooms
- 1/2 tsp cumin
- salt to taste
- ground cayenne pepper to taste
- 1 (15 oz.) can black beans, drained
- 1 (4 oz.) can diced green chile peppers, drained
- 1/3 C. shredded carrots
- 2 C. shredded Swiss cheese

Directions

- Boil your broth and veggies, once everything is boiling place a lid on the pot, set the heat to low, and let the contents gently cook for 47 mins.
- Coat a baking dish with oil and then set your oven to 350 degrees before doing anything else.
- Stir fry your onions, until soft, in olive oil, for about 7 mins, then combine in: mushrooms, zucchini, and chicken along with some cayenne, cumin, and salt.
- Stir fry the mix until the chicken is fully done.
- Get a bowl, combine: half of the cheese, the rice, carrots, onions, chilies, zucchini, chilies, chicken, beans, and mushrooms.
- Pour all the contents into the baking dish and cook it all in the oven covered with foil for 32 mins then take off the foil and cook for 8 more mins.
- Let the casserole stand for 10 mins before plating.
- Enjoy.

Amount per serving (8 total)

Timing Information:

Preparation	15 m
Cooking	1 h 35 m
Total Time	1 h 50 m

Nutritional Information:

Calories	337 kcal
Fat	21 g
Carbohydrates	11.5g
Protein	25.3 g
Cholesterol	77 mg
Sodium	363 mg

* Percent Daily Values are based on a 2,000 calorie diet.

MEATY NO-MEAT BROWN RICE BAKE

Ingredients

- 1 C. brown rice
- 1 C. beef broth
- 1 (14.5 oz.) can chicken broth
- 1/4 C. butter, melted
- 1 tsp garlic salt
- 1 tsp seasoned salt

Directions

- Set your oven to 350 degrees before doing anything else.
- Get a baking dish and layer in it: rice, both broths, and butter.
- Top with: seasoned salt and garlic salt.
- Cook everything in the oven for 1 hr.
- Enjoy.

Amount per serving (8 total)

Timing Information:

Preparation	10 m
Cooking	1 h
Total Time	1 h 10 m

Nutritional Information:

Calories	140 kcal
Fat	6.5 g
Carbohydrates	18.3g
Protein	2.2 g
Cholesterol	15 mg
Sodium	482 mg

* Percent Daily Values are based on a 2,000 calorie diet.

Easy Louisiana Style Brown Rice

Ingredients

- 2 tbsps butter
- 8 oz. andouille sausage, cut into 1/4-inch slices
- 2 tbsps ground paprika
- 1 tbsp ground cumin
- 1/2 tsp cayenne pepper
- 1/2 C. diced tomatoes
- 1 large green bell pepper, diced
- 2 stalks celery, sliced 1/4 inch thick
- 4 green onions, thinly sliced
- 1 tsp salt
- 1 bay leaf
- 1 C. uncooked brown rice
- 3 C. chicken stock
- 1 lb large shrimp, peeled and deveined
- salt and ground black pepper to taste

Directions

- Stir fry your sausage in butter, in a big pot, until browned.
- Then add in: cayenne, cumin, and paprika.
- Cook for 2 more mins.

- Now combine in: salt, bay leaf, tomatoes, onions, pepper, and celery.
- Stir the contents and cook for 1 more min before adding the stock and rice.
- Get everything boiling and once it is boiling place a lid on the pot, set the heat to low, and let the contents cook for 47 mins.
- Add in the shrimp and let them cook for 7 mins before adding in some pepper and salt.
- Enjoy.

Amount per serving (4 total)

Timing Information:

Preparation	15 m
Cooking	1 h
Total Time	1 h 15 m

Nutritional Information:

Calories	495 kcal
Fat	25.2 g
Carbohydrates	37.3g
Protein	30.3 g
Cholesterol	221 mg
Sodium	1909 mg

* Percent Daily Values are based on a 2,000 calorie diet.

EASY MEXICAN STYLE BROWN RICE

Ingredients

- 2 C. cooked brown rice
- 1 (15 oz.) can kidney beans, rinsed and drained
- 1 (15 oz.) can black beans, rinsed and drained
- 1 (15.25 oz.) can whole kernel corn, drained
- 1 small onion, diced
- 1 green bell pepper, diced
- 2 jalapeno peppers, seeded and diced
- 1 lime, zested and juiced
- 1/4 C. chopped cilantro leaves
- 1 tsp minced garlic
- 1 1/2 tsps ground cumin
- salt to taste

Directions

- Get a bowl, combine: cumin, rice, garlic, beans, cilantro, corn, lime juice & zest, onions, jalapenos, and green peppers.
- Add in your preferred amount of pepper and salt and place the contents in the fridge for 60 mins then stir everything and serve.

- Enjoy.

Amount per serving (10 total)

Timing Information:

Preparation	
Cooking	20 m
Total Time	1 h 20 m

Nutritional Information:

Calories	124 kcal
Fat	1 g
Carbohydrates	26g
Protein	4.7 g
Cholesterol	0 mg
Sodium	220 mg

* Percent Daily Values are based on a 2,000 calorie diet.

BLACK BEAN AND RICE BURGERS (VEGETARIAN APPROVED)

Ingredients

- 1/2 C. uncooked brown rice
- 1 C. water
- 2 (16 oz.) cans black beans, rinsed and drained
- 1 green bell pepper, halved and seeded
- 1 onion, quartered
- 1/2 C. sliced mushrooms
- 6 cloves garlic, peeled
- 3/4 C. shredded mozzarella cheese
- 2 eggs
- 1 tbsp chili powder
- 1 tbsp ground cumin
- 1 tbsp garlic salt
- 1 tsp hot sauce
- 1/2 C. dry bread crumbs, or as needed

Directions

- Get your water and rice boiling, then place a lid on the pot, set the heat to low, and let the contents gently cook for 47 mins.
- Heat up your grill and cover the grate with foil.
- With a blender, process: garlic, bell pepper, mushrooms, and onions. Then place everything in a bowl.
- Now blend the mozzarella and the rice and add them to the same bowl
- Get a 2nd bowl, mash: black beans until paste like.
- Then add in the blended mix.
- Get a 3rb bowl, combine: beaten eggs, hot sauce, chili powder, garlic salt, and cumin.
- Add this to the beans and then mix in your bread crumbs.
- Shape the bean mix into 6 burgers then grill each for 7 mins per side.
- Enjoy the patties with sesame seed buns and some mayo.
- Enjoy.

Amount per serving (6 total)

Timing Information:

Preparation	25 m
Cooking	16 m
Total Time	41 m

Nutritional Information:

Calories	317 kcal
Fat	5.8 g
Carbohydrates	49.4g
Protein	18.2 g
Cholesterol	71 mg
Sodium	1704 mg

* Percent Daily Values are based on a 2,000 calorie diet.

WALNUTS, BROCCOLI, AND CHEDDAR BROWN RICE

Ingredients

- 1/2 C. chopped walnuts
- 1 tbsp butter
- 1 onion, chopped
- 1/2 tsp minced garlic
- 1 C. uncooked instant brown rice
- 1 C. vegetable broth
- 1 lb fresh broccoli florets
- 1/2 tsp salt
- 1/8 tsp ground black pepper
- 1 C. shredded Cheddar cheese

Directions

- Set your oven to 350 degrees before doing anything else.
- Get a baking dish and toast your nuts in the oven for 9 mins.
- Microwave the broccoli until soft, then add in some pepper and salt.

- Now stir fry your garlic and onions in butter for 4 mins then add in the broth and rice. Get everything boiling, then place a lid on the pot, and let the contents, gently cook over a lower level of heat for 9 mins.
- On each serving plate add a layer of rice, then some broccoli, then nuts, and finally some cheese.
- Enjoy.

Amount per serving (4 total)

Timing Information:

Preparation	15 m
Cooking	25 m
Total Time	40 m

Nutritional Information:

Calories	368 kcal
Fat	22.9 g
Carbohydrates	30.4g
Protein	15.1 g
Cholesterol	37 mg
Sodium	643 mg

* Percent Daily Values are based on a 2,000 calorie diet.

BUTTERY PARSLEY AND SHRIMP

Ingredients

- 1 C. brown rice
- 1 2/3 C. water
- 3 tbsps butter
- 3 tbsps olive oil
- 2 cloves garlic, minced
- 1/2 C. white wine
- 2 tbsps fresh lemon juice
- 1 1/2 lbs medium shrimp - peeled and deveined
- 1/4 C. chopped fresh flat-leaf parsley
- 1/2 tsp cornstarch

Directions

- Boil your water and rice. Once everything is boiling set the heat to low, and let the contents gently cook for 27 mins.
- Stir fry your garlic in butter for 4 mins then add the lemon juice and wine.
- Get the mix simmering then pour in the shrimp and cook for 8 mins. Now top everything with parsley and cook for 3 more mins.

- Grab your cornstarch and gradually pour it in while stirring and cooking for about 1 to 2 mins until you have made a thick sauce.
- Place your rice on a plate then top with the shrimp and sauce.
- Enjoy.

Amount per serving (4 total)

Timing Information:

Preparation	15 m
Cooking	20 m
Total Time	35 m

Nutritional Information:

Calories	551 kcal
Fat	23 g
Carbohydrates	40.2g
Protein	38.5 g
Cholesterol	282 mg
Sodium	322 mg

* Percent Daily Values are based on a 2,000 calorie diet.

ONIONS, CHICKEN, PEAS, AND GARLIC BROWN RICE

Ingredients

- 2 tbsps vegetable oil, divided
- 8 oz. skinless, boneless chicken breast, cut into strips
- 1/2 red bell pepper, chopped
- 1/2 C. green onion, chopped
- 4 cloves garlic, minced
- 3 C. cooked brown rice
- 2 tbsps light soy sauce
- 1 tbsp rice vinegar
- 1 C. frozen peas, thawed

Directions

- Stir fry your garlic, chicken, onions, and bell peppers in half of the veggie oil for 7 mins or until the chicken is fully done.
- Place the chicken mix to the side.
- Add in the rest of the oil and toast your rice in it for 1 min then add: peas, vinegar, and soy sauce.
- Cook for 2 more mins and add back in the chicken.

- Once everything is heated through you can serve it.
- Enjoy.

Amount per serving (3 total)

Timing Information:

Preparation	20 m
Cooking	15 m
Total Time	35 m

Nutritional Information:

Calories	486 kcal
Fat	13.7 g
Carbohydrates	57.4g
Protein	32.1 g
Cholesterol	64 mg
Sodium	720 mg

* Percent Daily Values are based on a 2,000 calorie diet.

EGGPLANT, BASIL, FETA SANDWICH

Ingredients

- 1 small eggplant, halved and sliced
- 1 tbsp olive oil, or as needed
- 1/4 C. mayonnaise
- 2 cloves garlic, minced
- 2 (6 inch) French sandwich rolls
- 1 small tomato, sliced
- 1/2 C. crumbled feta cheese
- 1/4 C. minced fresh basil leaves

Directions

- Turn on your broiler to low if possible.
- Get a bowl, mix: garlic and mayo.
- Take your eggplant pieces and coat them with olive oil. Put them on a sheet for baking.
- For 10 mins cook the eggplant in the broiler 6 inches from the heat.
- Cut your French bread in half and toast it.
- Spread a good amount of mayo and garlic mix on your bread and layer the following to form a sandwich: tomato, basil leaves, eggplant, and feta.

- Enjoy.

Amount per serving (2 total)

Timing Information:

Preparation	Cooking	Total Time
20 m	10 m	30 m

Nutritional Information:

Calories	802 kcal
Fat	39.5 g
Carbohydrates	91.3g
Protein	23.8 g
Cholesterol	44 mg
Sodium	1460 mg

* Percent Daily Values are based on a 2,000 calorie diet.

Balsamic Mushroom Sandwich

Ingredients

- 2 cloves garlic, minced
- 6 tbsps olive oil
- 1/2 tsp dried thyme
- 2 tbsps balsamic vinegar
- salt and pepper to taste
- 4 large Portobello mushroom caps
- 4 hamburger buns
- 1 tbsp capers
- 1/4 C. mayonnaise
- 1 tbsp capers, drained
- 1 large tomato, sliced
- 4 leaves lettuce

Directions

- Preheat your broiler and set its rack so that it is near the heating source before doing anything else.
- Get a bowl and mix: pepper, garlic, salt, olive oil, vinegar, and thyme.
- Get a 2nd bowl, combine: mayo and capers.
- Coat your mushrooms with half of the dressing.

- Then toast the veggies for 5 mins under the broiler.
- Flip the mushrooms after coating the opposite side with the remaining dressing.
- Toast everything for 5 more mins.
- Now also toast your bread.
- Apply some mayo to the bread before layering a mushroom, some lettuce and tomato.
- Enjoy.

Amount per serving (4 total)

Timing Information:

Preparation	Cooking	Total Time
8 m	9 m	20 m

Nutritional Information:

Calories	445 kcal
Fat	33.4 g
Carbohydrates	31.4g
Protein	7.8 g
Cholesterol	5 mg
Sodium	426 mg

* Percent Daily Values are based on a 2,000 calorie diet.

MEATBALL MADNESS SANDWICH

Ingredients

- 1 lb ground beef
- 3/4 C. bread crumbs
- 2 tsps dried Italian seasoning
- 2 cloves garlic, minced
- 2 tbsps minced fresh parsley
- 2 tbsps grated Parmesan cheese
- 1 egg, beaten
- 1 French baguette
- 1 tbsp extra-virgin olive oil
- 1/2 tsp garlic powder
- 1 pinch salt, or to taste
- 1 (14 oz.) jar spaghetti sauce
- 4 slices provolone cheese

Directions

- Set your oven to 350 degrees before doing anything else.
- Get a bowl, combine: eggs, beef, parmesan, bread crumbs, parsley, garlic, and Italian seasoning.
- Mold the mix into your preferred size of meatballs and cook them in the oven for 22 mins.

- Now cut your bread and take out some of the inside so the meatballs fit better.
- Toast the bread for 6 mins in the oven after coating it with some olive oil, salt, and garlic powder.
- Get a saucepan and heat up your pasta sauce.
- Add in your meatballs to the sauce after they are cooked and mix everything.
- Put some meatballs into your bread and then toast the sandwich in the oven for 4 mins before serving.
- Enjoy.

Amount per serving (4 total)

Timing Information:

Preparation	Cooking	Total Time
20 m	20 m	40 m

Nutritional Information:

Calories	781 kcal
Fat	31.9 g
Carbohydrates	78.2g
Protein	43.6 g
Cholesterol	141 mg
Sodium	1473 mg

* Percent Daily Values are based on a 2,000 calorie diet.

THE SPRING TIME SANDWICH

Ingredients

- 1/2 C. mayonnaise
- 1/4 C. blue cheese dressing
- 8 slices multigrain bread
- 2 cooked chicken breasts, sliced
- 1 ripe avocado, sliced
- 8 slices cooked bacon
- 2 hard-boiled eggs, minced
- 4 lettuce leaves

Directions

- Get a bowl and mix the blue cheese with some mayo.
- Coat your bread with 2 tbsps of this mix.
- Place a quarter of your chicken breast on four pieces of bread.
- Then layer the following on each piece: lettuce, avocado, hard-boiled egg, bacon, another piece of bread.
- Enjoy with some blue cheese on the side for dipping.

Amount per serving (4 total)

Timing Information:

Preparation	Cooking	Total Time
25 m		25 m

Nutritional Information:

Calories	811 kcal
Fat	56.1 g
Carbohydrates	29.6g
Protein	46.3 g
Cholesterol	204 mg
Sodium	908 mg

* Percent Daily Values are based on a 2,000 calorie diet.

THE FLUFFY SANDWICH

Ingredients

- 2 tbsps peanut butter
- 2 slices bread
- 2 1/2 tbsps marshmallow cream

Directions

- Lay two pieces of bread flat on a working surface.
- Coat one piece of bread with peanut butter, and another piece with marshmallow cream.
- Now microwave the pieces of bread for 30 secs with the highest power setting.
- Form the pieces into a sandwich and enjoy with milk.

Amount per serving (1 total)

Timing Information:

Preparation	Cooking	Total Time
4 m	1 m	5 m

Nutritional Information:

Calories	373 kcal
Fat	18.1 g
Carbohydrates	43.5g
Protein	12.1 g
Cholesterol	0 mg
Sodium	502 mg

* Percent Daily Values are based on a 2,000 calorie diet.

PEPPERONCINI SANDWICH

Ingredients

- 2 thick slices whole wheat bread
- 2 tbsps cream cheese, softened
- 6 slices cucumber
- 2 tbsps alfalfa sprouts
- 1 tsp olive oil
- 1 tsp red wine vinegar
- 1 tomato, sliced
- 1 leaf lettuce
- 1 oz. pepperoncini, sliced
- 1/2 avocado, mashed

Directions

- Layer one piece of bread with the following: 1 tbsp of cream cheese, alfalfa sprouts, oil and vinegar, cucumber pieces, tomatoes, pepperoncini, and lettuce.
- Coat another piece of bread with avocado and form a sandwich.
- Enjoy.

Amount per serving (1 total)

Timing Information:

Preparation	Cooking	Total Time
10 m		10 m

Nutritional Information:

Calories	496 kcal
Fat	32.5 g
Carbohydrates	46.3g
Protein	11.4 g
Cholesterol	32 mg
Sodium	1024 mg

* Percent Daily Values are based on a 2,000 calorie diet.

LUNCH BOX ITALIAN STYLE SANDWICH

Ingredients

- 1 (1 lb) loaf fresh Italian bread
- 1/3 C. olive oil
- 1/3 C. grated Parmesan cheese
- 1 tbsp dried basil
- 1 tbsp dried oregano
- 8 oil-cured black olives, pitted and minced
- 8 pitted green olives, minced
- 1/4 lb thinly sliced salami
- 1/4 lb thinly sliced ham
- 1/2 lb provolone cheese, sliced
- 1/4 lb mozzarella cheese, sliced

Directions

- Cut your bread in half then coat one side with: olive oil, oregano, parmesan, and basil.
- Add the following to the other piece: green olives, mozzarella, black olives, provolone, ham and salami.
- Form everything into a sandwich and divide it into multiple pieces.
- Enjoy.

Amount per serving (4 total)

Timing Information:

Preparation	Cooking	Total Time
15 m		15 m

Nutritional Information:

Calories	975 kcal
Fat	59.9 g
Carbohydrates	61.3g
Protein	46.2 g
Cholesterol	107 mg
Sodium	2790 mg

* Percent Daily Values are based on a 2,000 calorie diet.

SUMMER SANDWICH

Ingredients

- 1 (1 lb) loaf ciabatta bread
- 3/4 C. pesto
- 8 oz. fontina cheese, sliced
- 2 ripe tomatoes, sliced
- 4 leaves butter lettuce

Directions

- Turn on your oven's broiler to low if possible.
- Cut your bread in half. Coat one side with some pesto then layer the following on the other side: tomato, and fontina cheese.
- Place the pieces of bread which have cheese under the broiler until the cheese has melted.
- Top this piece with some lettuce.
- Form sandwiches then cut them in half for serving.
- Enjoy.

Amount per serving (8 total)

Timing Information:

Preparation	Cooking	Total Time
15 m	5 m	20 m

Nutritional Information:

Calories	386 kcal
Fat	21.5 g
Carbohydrates	31.6g
Protein	16.8 g
Cholesterol	40 mg
Sodium	738 mg

* Percent Daily Values are based on a 2,000 calorie diet.

EASY EUROPEAN SANDWICH

Ingredients

- 1 (8 oz.) package cream cheese, softened
- 1/2 C. butter, softened
- 1 tbsp minced garlic
- 2 loaves French bread, sliced
- 1 lb sliced sausage of your choice
- 1 cucumber, sliced
- 3 medium tomatoes, sliced
- 1 hard-cooked egg, minced

Directions

- Get a bowl, mix: garlic, butter, and cream cheese.
- Coat a piece of bread with this mix.
- Then layer the following on each bread piece: tomato, sausage, cucumber, egg.
- Enjoy this sandwich open.

Amount per serving (25 total)

Timing Information:

Preparation	Cooking	Total Time
15 m		15 m

Nutritional Information:

Calories	233 kcal
Fat	12.9 g
Carbohydrates	21.9g
Protein	7.7 g
Cholesterol	39 mg
Sodium	470 mg

* Percent Daily Values are based on a 2,000 calorie diet.

THE BROOKLYN STYLE SANDWICH

Ingredients

- 3 C. shredded cabbage
- 2 tbsps vegetable oil
- 2 tbsps apple cider vinegar
- 2 tbsps white sugar
- 1 tsp adobo seasoning
- 1 tsp ground black pepper
- 4 C. vegetable oil for frying
- 3 whole russet potatoes
- 8 thick slices Italian bread
- 1 lb sliced pastrami (divided)
- 4 slices provolone cheese
- 8 slices tomato

Directions

- Get a bowl and combine evenly: black pepper, cabbage, adobo, veggie oil (2 tbsps), sugar, and vinegar.
- Get a large pot and get your oil to 375 degrees then set your oven to 225 degrees before doing anything else.
- Dice your potatoes into slices and fry them in the oil for 6 mins.

- Now place the potatoes to the side.
- For 6 mins toast your bread in the oven.
- On 4 slices of bread layer: pastrami and cheese.
- Now toast the pieces for 4 more mins to melt the cheese.
- Layer the following on the pastrami: 2 tomato pieces, cabbage mix, fried potatoes, and another piece of toasted bread.
- Enjoy.

Amount per serving (4 total)

Timing Information:

Preparation	Cooking	Total Time
30 m	15 m	45 m

Nutritional Information:

Calories	892 kcal
Fat	45.3 g
Carbohydrates	79.5g
Protein	42.7 g
Cholesterol	97 mg
Sodium	1604 mg

* Percent Daily Values are based on a 2,000 calorie diet.

TEMPEH SANDWICH

(VEGETARIAN APPROVED)

Ingredients

- 1 tbsp sesame oil
- 1 (8 oz.) package tempeh, sliced into thin strips
- 2 tbsps liquid amino acid supplement
- 1 tbsp sesame oil
- 1 small onion, thinly sliced
- 1 medium green bell pepper, thinly sliced
- 1 jalapeno pepper, sliced
- 2 pita breads, cut in half
- soy mayonnaise
- 4 thin slices Swiss cheese

Directions

- For 5 mins fry your tempeh in hot oil, add half of the amino's liquid, then cook everything for 2 more mins.
- Flip all the tempeh pieces and continue frying them for another 2 mins.
- Now add the rest of the amino's liquid and cook the mix for 2 more mins.

- Place everything to the side.
- Stir fry your jalapenos, onions, and green peppers for 6 mins with fresh oil in the same pan.
- Coat each piece of pita with some mayo (1 tsp).
- Then fill each piece with some onion mix, tempeh, and Swiss cheese.
- For 2 mins toast the pita in a toaster oven or on the stove until the Swiss melts.
- Enjoy.

Amount per serving (4 total)

Timing Information:

Preparation	Cooking	Total Time
10 m	20 m	30 m

Nutritional Information:

Calories	392 kcal
Fat	24.8 g
Carbohydrates	24.4g
Protein	21.7 g
Cholesterol	28 mg
Sodium	551 mg

* Percent Daily Values are based on a 2,000 calorie diet.

EASY EGG AND AMERICAN SANDWICH

Ingredients

- 1 egg
- 1 tbsp milk
- 2 slices white bread
- salt and pepper to taste (optional)
- 1 slice American cheese

Directions

- Get a bowl, and mix: whisked eggs, salt, pepper, and milk.
- Microwave the mix for 90 secs in the microwave with the highest power setting.
- Simultaneously toast your bread slices then add your egg to the toasted bread.
- Before forming a sandwich top the egg with a piece of cheese.
- Now heat everything in the microwave for 30 more secs.
- Enjoy.

Amount per serving (1 total)

Timing Information:

Preparation	Cooking	Total Time
1 m	4 m	5 m

Nutritional Information:

Calories	318 kcal
Fat	15.8 g
Carbohydrates	26.9g
Protein	16.9 g
Cholesterol	214 mg
Sodium	839 mg

* Percent Daily Values are based on a 2,000 calorie diet.

TURKEY CLUB

Ingredients

- 1 (16 oz.) package frozen bite-size potato nuggets (such as Tater Tots(R)), or as needed
- 2 slices deli ham, or more to taste
- 2 slices deli turkey, or more to taste
- 1 tomato slice
- 10 potato chips (such as Lay's(R)), or more to taste
- 4 slices cooked bacon
- 1 slice Swiss cheese, or more to taste
- 4 pickle slices

Directions

- Cook half of your tater tots in a heated waffle maker for about 5 mins with the lid down. Then continue cooking the remaining pieces of potatoes.
- Now layer some of the tater tots on a serving plate to serve as bread then top it with: turkey, ham, tomato, and chips.
- Finally add Swiss, pickles, and bacon.
- Now place the rest of your tater tots to form the top piece of bread.
- Enjoy.

Amount per serving (1 total)

Timing Information:

Preparation	Cooking	Total Time
10 m	10 m	20 m

Nutritional Information:

Calories	1230 kcal
Fat	71.1 g
Carbohydrates	126.1g
Protein	46.9 g
Cholesterol	107 mg
Sodium	4245 mg

* Percent Daily Values are based on a 2,000 calorie diet.

TUNA SANDWICH DONE RIGHT

Ingredients

- 1 (6 oz.) can tuna, drained
- 1/4 C. mayonnaise
- 1 1/2 tsps cream-style horseradish sauce
- 1 tbsp chopped dill pickles
- 2 leaves lettuce
- 2 slices Swiss cheese
- 4 slices bread
- 2 slices tomato
- 2 thin slices red onion

Directions

- Get a bowl, combine: pickles, tuna, horseradish, and mayo. Stir the mix until it even and smooth.
- Top 2 pieces of bread with 1 piece of Swiss and a piece of lettuce. Evenly divide your tuna mix between the bread slices then layer your onions and tomatoes.
- Place the other piece of bread to make a sandwich.
- Enjoy.

Amount per serving (2 total)

Timing Information:

Preparation	Cooking	Total Time
	15 m	15 m

Nutritional Information:

Calories	553 kcal
Fat	32.9 g
Carbohydrates	30.2g
Protein	33.7 g
Cholesterol	63 mg
Sodium	656 mg

* Percent Daily Values are based on a 2,000 calorie diet.

Tuna Lunch Burritos

Ingredients

- 2 (6 oz.) cans tuna, drained
- 3 tbsp mayonnaise
- 1 1/2 tbsp pickle relish
- 1 tbsp chopped onion
- 1 tbsp chopped celery
- 1 tsp lemon juice, or to taste
- 1 pinch garlic salt, or to taste
- 4 leaves lettuce (optional)
- 4 (8 inch) flour tortillas, warmed

Directions

- In a bowl, mix together the tuna, mayonnaise, pickle relish, onion, celery, lemon juice and garlic salt.
- Arrange 1 lettuce leaf over each tortilla and place the tuna mixture in a line across the middle of each tortilla.
- Fold opposing edges of the tortilla to overlap the filling and roll 1 of the opposing edges around the filling in a burrito-style.

Amount per serving (4 total)

Timing Information:

Preparation	
Cooking	10 m
Total Time	10 m

Nutritional Information:

Calories	341 kcal
Fat	12.4 g
Carbohydrates	30.2g
Protein	25.9 g
Cholesterol	29 mg
Sodium	465 mg

* Percent Daily Values are based on a 2,000 calorie diet.

TUNA CHEESE BURGERS

Ingredients

- 3 eggs
- 1/4 lb. processed cheese food, diced
- 2 tbsp sweet pickle relish
- 1 (6 oz.) can tuna, drained
- 2 tbsp minced onion
- 1/2 C. creamy salad dressing, e.g. Miracle Whip (TM)
- 3 tbsp chopped stuffed green olives
- 4 hamburger buns

Directions

- Set your oven to 400 degrees F before doing anything else.
- In a pan of cold water, add the eggs. Bring to a boil and immediately remove from the heat.
- Keep aside the eggs, covered in hot water for about 10-12 minutes.
- Remove from the hot water and keep aside to cool.
- Peel the eggs and then chop.
- In a large bowl, add the eggs, processed cheese food, sweet pickle relish, tuna, onion, creamy salad dressing and green olives and mix completely.

- Spread the mixture over the hamburger buns and wrap in foil paper.
- Cook in the oven for about 15 minutes.

Amount per serving (4 total)

Timing Information:

Preparation	15 m
Cooking	15 m
Total Time	30 m

Nutritional Information:

Calories	427 kcal
Fat	21.9 g
Carbohydrates	31.2g
Protein	25.3 g
Cholesterol	180 mg
Sodium	1045 mg

* Percent Daily Values are based on a 2,000 calorie diet.

SATISFYING TUNA SANDWICH

Ingredients

- 1 (10.75 oz.) can condensed cream of mushroom soup
- 2 hard-cooked eggs, sliced
- 1 (6 oz.) can tuna, drained
- 6 slices whole wheat bread

Directions

- Prepare the cream of mushroom soup according to the directions on the can.
- Stir in the canned tuna and egg slices and cook till heated completely.
- Meanwhile, toast the bread slices.
- Spread the tuna mixture over the toasted slices and serve.

Amount per serving (3 total)

Timing Information:

Preparation	5 m
Cooking	25 m
Total Time	30 m

Nutritional Information:

Calories	333 kcal
Fat	11.9 g
Carbohydrates	32g
Protein	24.5 g
Cholesterol	158 mg
Sodium	994 mg

* Percent Daily Values are based on a 2,000 calorie diet.

HOW TO MAKE A TUNA MELT

Ingredients

- 1 (1 lb.) loaf French bread
- 1 small sweet onion, peeled and diced
- 1 (12 oz.) can tuna, drained
- 2 C. mozzarella cheese, shredded
- 1 C. mayonnaise

Directions

- Set your oven to 350 degrees F before doing anything else.
- In a bowl, add the sweet onion, drained tuna, mozzarella and mayonnaise and mix till well combined.
- Spread the tuna mixture over the French bread slices to form a sandwich.
- Arrange the sandwiches onto a cookie sheet.
- Cook in the oven for about 10 minutes.

Amount per serving (8 total)

Timing Information:

Preparation	15 m
Cooking	10 m
Total Time	25 m

Nutritional Information:

Calories	483 kcal
Fat	27.7 g
Carbohydrates	34.1g
Protein	24.5 g
Cholesterol	41 mg
Sodium	716 mg

* Percent Daily Values are based on a 2,000 calorie diet.

Shibuya Terminal Tuna

Ingredients

- 1 C. teriyaki sauce
- 3/4 C. olive oil
- 2 tbsp minced garlic
- 1 tsp ground black pepper
- 4 (4 oz.) fillets yellowfin tuna

Directions

- In a large resealable plastic bag, mix together the teriyaki sauce, oil, garlic and pepper.
- Add the tuna fillets and seal the bag with as little air in it as possible.
- Shake well to coat the tuna fillets with marinade.
- Refrigerate to marinade for about 30 minutes.
- Set your outdoor grill for high heat and lightly, grease the grill grate.
- Remove the tuna from marinade.
- Cook the tuna fillets on grill for about 3-5 minutes per side.

Amount per serving (4 total)

Timing Information:

Preparation	5 m
Cooking	10 m
Total Time	45 m

Nutritional Information:

Calories	551 kcal
Fat	41.6 g
Carbohydrates	12.9g
Protein	30.7 g
Cholesterol	51 mg
Sodium	2803 mg

* Percent Daily Values are based on a 2,000 calorie diet.

PEPPERY CAYENNE TUNA

Ingredients

- 2 (5 oz.) ahi tuna steaks
- 1 tsp kosher salt
- 1/4 tsp cayenne pepper
- 1/2 tbsp butter
- 2 tbsp olive oil
- 1 tsp whole peppercorns

Directions

- Season the tuna steaks with the salt and cayenne pepper.
- In a skillet, heat the olive oil and butter on medium-high heat and cook the peppercorns for about 5 minutes.
- Gently place the seasoned tuna in the skillet and cook for about 1 1/2 minutes per side.

Amount per serving (2 total)

Timing Information:

Preparation	5 m
Cooking	12 m
Total Time	17 m

Nutritional Information:

Calories	301 kcal
Fat	17.8 g
Carbohydrates	0.7g
Protein	33.3 g
Cholesterol	71 mg
Sodium	1034 mg

* Percent Daily Values are based on a 2,000 calorie diet.

MEXICO CITY SANDWICH

Ingredients

- 1 (1 lb.) loaf French bread
- 10 oz. ahi (yellowfin) tuna, sushi-grade - sliced 1 inch long and 1/8 inch thick
- 1/4 C. onion, cut into 1/8-inch dice
- 2 tbsp capers, drained
- 3 oz. olive oil
- 3 tbsp fresh lemon juice
- 1 tsp kosher salt
- 1/4 tsp freshly ground black pepper

Directions

- Cut the French bread into 1/4 inch thick slices and keep aside.
- In a flat nonreactive dish, arrange the tuna slices in a single layer and top with the onion and capers.
- Drizzle with the olive oil and lemon juice and sprinkle with the kosher salt and black pepper.
- Serve tuna slices over French bread slices.

Amount per serving (5 total)

Timing Information:

Preparation	30 m
Cooking	30 m
Total Time	30 m

Nutritional Information:

Calories	477 kcal
Fat	19.3 g
Carbohydrates	52.3g
Protein	24 g
Cholesterol	26 mg
Sodium	1090 mg

* Percent Daily Values are based on a 2,000 calorie diet.

ALL AMERICAN OMELET

Ingredients

- 2 tsp vegetable oil
- 1/2 small onion, chopped
- 1 (6 oz.) can tuna, drained
- 1/3 C. sour cream
- 3 tbsp cream cheese
- 1/2 C. shredded mozzarella cheese
- 1 (2.25 oz.) can sliced black olives
- 1/8 tsp dried dill weed
- 1/8 tsp garlic powder
- 5 eggs
- 1/4 C. milk
- 2 tsp vegetable oil

Directions

- In a large skillet, heat 2 tsp of the vegetable oil on medium heat and sauté the onion till the onion just begins to brown.
- In a large bowl, add the tuna, sour cream, cream cheese, mozzarella cheese, olives, dill, garlic powder and cooked onion and mix well.
- In another large bowl, add the eggs and milk and beat.

- In the same skillet used to cook the onion, heat 2 tsp of the oil and place the egg mixture.
- As eggs set, lift the edges to let the liquid to run underneath evenly.
- After the eggs are almost set, place the tuna mixture over one half of the eggs and fold the other half over the filling.
- Cover the skillet and immediately, remove from the heat.
- Keep the skillet, covered till the cheese melts.

Amount per serving (2 total)

Timing Information:

Preparation	10 m
Cooking	10 m
Total Time	20 m

Nutritional Information:

Calories	
Fat	
Carbohydrates	
Protein	
Cholesterol	
Sodium	

* Percent Daily Values are based on a 2,000 calorie diet.

MONDAY'S PITA SANDWICH

Ingredients

- 1/2 pita bread round
- 1/4 C. tuna, drained
- 1/2 dill pickle spear, diced
- 1 1/2 tsp mayonnaise
- 1 1/2 tsp olive oil
- 1/2 tsp garlic powder
- 1 pinch dried rosemary
- 1 slice Swiss cheese

Directions

- Lightly toast the pita bread.
- Break tuna chunks into small pieces and place into a bowl.
- Add the pickle, mayonnaise, olive oil, garlic powder and rosemary and mix till well combined.
- Place Swiss cheese into the pocket of the toasted pita bread, followed by the tuna mixture.
- In a microwave safe dish, place the pita sandwich and microwave for about 15-20 seconds.

Amount per serving (1 total)

Timing Information:

Preparation	10 m
Cooking	5 m
Total Time	15 m

Nutritional Information:

Calories	394 kcal
Fat	21.6 g
Carbohydrates	20.7g
Protein	28.4 g
Cholesterol	49 mg
Sodium	482 mg

* Percent Daily Values are based on a 2,000 calorie diet.

THANKS FOR READING! JOIN THE CLUB AND KEEP ON COOKING WITH 6 MORE COOKBOOKS....

http://bit.ly/1TdrStv

To grab the box sets simply follow the link mentioned above, or tap one of book covers.

This will take you to a page where you can simply enter your email address and a PDF version of the box sets will be emailed to you.

Hope you are ready for some serious cooking!

http://bit.ly/1TdrStv

COME ON...
LET'S BE FRIENDS :)

We adore our readers and love connecting with them socially.

Like BookSumo on Facebook and let's get social!

Facebook

And also check out the BookSumo Cooking Blog.

Food Lover Blog

16375426R00094

Printed in Poland
by Amazon Fulfillment
Poland Sp. z o.o., Wrocław